Forever Seems Too Long

Jo Ann Atcheson Gray

Copyright © [2024] by [Jo Ann Atcheson Gray]

All rights reserved.

No portion of this book may be reproduced in any form without written permission from the publisher or author, except as permitted by U.S. copyright law.

Published by Jo Ann Gray

Contents

Forever Seems Too Long   1

Forever Seems Too Long   2

Fullpage image   17

Fullpage image   18

Forever Seems Too Long

Forever Seems Too Long

A party can be fun, yet it can lead to a disaster. I'm Scarlett Anne. I am now an immortal, a vampire. Me and Olivia stood at the entrance of The Catacombs, a small, underground venue in the heart of the city, hidden deep, and famous for its intimate, dark yet gritty atmosphere. The neon sign outside glowed in a sickly red hue, the letters flickering slightly as if they could give out any second. A long line of people, mostly dressed in black leather and faded denim, snaked around the building, buzzing with anticipation. Tonight was no ordinary rock show, Bloody Stains, a cult-favorite band with a reputation for electrifying live performances, was about to take the stage. Olivia and I had been excited for weeks, waiting for this opportunity, this rock show, and if the rumors were true, their lead guitarist, Brian, was more than just your typical rockstar.

This was the very first show, the first time getting to see this band 'live' and we couldn't wait to see them perform. Me, with my wild hair, my wild dark curls dyed temporarily with red, crimson at the tips, and Olivia, dressed in black with her signature, fake purple streaks, exchanging excited, yet nervous, glances. We had been waiting forever it seemed for this night to arrive, Bloody Stains didn't perform here too often, but it's said that when they do, it was an experience that the crowd would always leave in an amazed trance, something enchanting.

As we finally entered the venue, the air hit us with a dense mixture of sweat, cigarettes, and the aroma of alcohol, along with the low hum of the opening band's instruments that were obviously being tuned. The stage at the far end of the massive room was shrouded in the darkness, but we could see the faint shadows of the band members moving about, getting ready for the rock show. The noisy crowd around us buzzed with a restless energy, and I could feel it thrumming through my veins, like the pulsing beat of a song that hadn't even started yet.

"Do you think the rumors are true, Scarlett Anne," Olivia asked, her voice screaming above the crowd, "I mean, what if they are?"

I grinned, my eyes gleaming under the dim lights, as I screamed back in response, "About Brian? Absolutely! I mean, I hope they are... There's no way any human being could play the guitar like that without being supernatural." We both laughed, our echo fading into the loud crowd.

Olivia smirked as she sipped her drink, yet she did not argue my response. The music scene was full of eccentric characters that swarmed all around us, but this Brian guy, was strangely different. He was tall, with very pale skin and jet-black hair, he had an estranged magnetism that was impossible to ignore, or at least, he seemed this way on the television. His fingers always seemed to dance across his guitar strings, as if they were magically enchanted, and then there were all the whispers, the mere rumors, of how no one ever seen him in the daylight hours, of how his eyes glowed a strange crimson during performances, of how people left his shows with mysterious bite marks on their necks. And Olivia and I was about to see this for ourselves.

The lights suddenly dimmed, got much darker, and the crowd erupted in screams and cheers. Me and Olivia pushed our way to the front, the press of sweaty bodies all around us seemed to tighten as everyone surged forward toward the stage. A low, distorted musical note hummed from the massive speakers next to us, and the stage was bathed in a deep red light, swirling in circles. Bloody Stains had arrived and was about to perform.

The drummer pounded a slow, thunderous beat, and the bassist's fingers moved with raw, primal intensity, as the faint, thin veil dropped, the music soaring through the venue. The stage lit up, revealing the performers in full aspect, but I knew all eyes were on Brian, the lead guitarist, as he stepped forward. He was as striking in person as the rumors and social media had suggested. He was tall and gaunt, with cheekbones sharp enough to cut glass. His black leather jacket clung to him like a second skin, and his eyes, oh, his eyes, gleamed like fire in the dim lighting. When he strummed the first chord, it sent shivers down my spine. The mere sound was like nothing I'd ever heard before, raw and feral, a sound that seemed to reach deep into my chest and take hold of my mere heartbeat. The rowdy crowd swayed, moved as one, a sea of bodies swaying and pulsing to the rhythm, but I felt like I was the only one standing in front of the stage, like Brian's music was meant just for me.

Olivia leaned in close, shouting over the music, "This is unreal!"

I only nodded, unable to really hear her, unable to tear my eyes away from the man on the stage. I could feel the energy crackling in the heavy air, something electric, something... alive, or 'undead', I smirked to myself at the mere thought. As Brian's solo began in full, it was as if the world tilted on its axis. His pale fingers moved with a supernatural speed, his hands blurring across the strings of his guitar in a display of raw, dirty talent, mingled with a hint of some kind of dark magic. My heart raced in my chest, my blood pumping in time with the loud music. Brian's mystic eyes swept over the crowd as he grinned an enchanting grin, and for a moment, I swear, they locked onto mine. Time seemed to slow down, his mere gaze was so predatory, intense, and I felt an icy chill run down my spine. 'Was it fear, or something else?' I thought to myself. Whatever it was, it was so intoxicating.

As the rock song reached its climax, Brian tilted his head back, tossing his long hair over his shoulders, baring his throat for only a second, and as he smiled again, I could have sworn I saw the flash of fangs. The rumors were true, I suppose, he really had fangs in his mouth. Brian really was a vampire, or at least, he really pretended to be one. This realization should've terrified me, but instead, it thrilled me even more.

The lights pulsed, and Brian's guitar seemed to wail with a sound that was not entirely of this world. I could feel the loud music deep inside my bones, vibrating through my skull, echoing in my veins. It was almost too much to bear, but I did not want it to stop. Olivia was jumping and screaming, happily, when I shot a small glance her way, as she jumped next to me in beat with the crowd. By the time the final note rang out, the massive crowd seemed to be in a frenzy. Loud screams, cheers, and wild applause echoed through the venue. Brian, up on the stage still holding his guitar, gave a small, knowing smirk and backed away into the shadows, leaving the stage in a swirl of mist, as if he had never been there at all.

Me and Olivia stood in stunned silence for a moment, as the crowd made their exit, the mere energy of the performance still lingering in the air around us.

"That was... so insane!" Olivia finally screeched, nearly breathless.

I nodded in agreement, my thoughts racing, "Olivia, he looked right at me."

Olivia raised an eyebrow, "Scarlett Anne, he was looking at everyone."

"No," I insisted, my voice steady, "It was differnt. I felt... something. It was like he knew I was staring only at him, like he looked straight into my soul."

Olivia gave me a curious look but shrugged, "Maybe he did, Scarlet Anne, or maybe, you just got hypnotized like everyone else in this place. The rumors said that you would leave feeling enchanted."

Just shaking my head with no response, we made our way outside the venue into the cool night air, the sound of the city still buzzing all around us, but I still could not shake the estranged feeling that the night wasn't exactly over. Something in me felt changed. The music, the mere power, the tempting look that was in Brian's mystic eyes... it had awakened something inside me, something that felt dark, confusing, something that seemed wild. As we walked down the busy street, I glanced back at the venue, half expecting to see Brian watching me from the shadows. It was a surreal feeling. I felt a strange pull, a faint connection that I couldn't quite explain, and though the rock show was over, I knew this was just a beginning... of what, I was not quite sure, but it was a feeling that something was definitely different.

So, it was true, the mere rumor of this guitarist leaving his enchanted mark. He had definitely left something on me, this vampire guitarist, that I could not shake my thoughts from.

In the heart of New Orleans, where the air thrummed with jazz and the scent of sweet jasmine clung to the evening mist, I danced through the shadows of the French Quarter. With my petite frame and cascading black, curly hair, I moved like a faint whisper among the vibrant throngs of people. My brown eyes sparkled with much mischief, framed by the soft glow of all the neon lights. It was 1995, and the city pulsed with life, the night a living tapestry of music on every corner, much laughter, and many secrets waiting to be uncovered. Olivia and I explored every inch of the night life this city had to offer. We moved here to the French Quarter almost a year ago from Virginia, straight out of high school. We wanted to start our own lives and live on our own, away from our families and our parents' control, away from their rules. Just barely legal enough to enter the local bars and venues, we quickly learned the proper language of the bar scene. We were enjoying a life of freedom amongst ourselves and living the way we thought best.

Sharing my small apartment with my chaotic best friend, Olivia, a striking blonde with emerald-green eyes that seemed to capture every flicker of light. Our tiny two-bedroom dwelling was a whirlwind of posters from our favorite rock bands, empty bottles, and the remnants of late-night adventures from many rock shows. The mere walls vibrated with the echoes of various rock ballads and the smell of popcorn from movie marathons that turned into early-morning discussions about life and love, along with many conversations of pointless information about our favorite rock artists. Every Friday night, the two of us would paint our lips a bold red, our eyes as black as night, lace up our combat boots, and set out to follow various bands, especially Bloody Stains, the mere band that had captured our hearts and souls.

It had been several months, but Bloody Stains, the European rock band, had returned to the French Quarter. The air buzzed with our excited anticipation as we arrived at the bar, one that was tucked deep into the outskirts of the Quarter. The sound of the small crowd was a roaring wave of mere excitement, but it was Brian, the enigmatic lead guitarist with his dark, flowing hair and hypnotic, hollow eyes, that sent my heart racing. He possessed an estranged magnetism that just drew me in every time I watched him, a power that made me feel strangely alive in a way I had never experienced. As the first chords of Bloody Stains filled the air in the small venue, I felt the world around dissolve. Each musical note wrapped around me, pulling me deeper into a spiral of much passion and longing. Brian was a force of nature, it seemed, as he played his guitar on the stage in front of Olivia and me, wailing it like a siren. It was completely impossible not to be captivated. I found myself totally entranced, lost in his performance, forgetting the boundary between a fan and something unknown, something more. Of course, Olivia thought I was being obsessed, insane, but she just laughed it off.

After the rock show had ended, Olivia and I had won backstage passes... 'meet and greet' from the radio station. I felt like our connection ignited even more after the electrifying show, as Brian's presence was intoxicating, his mere smile a challenge I could not resist. We exchanged playful banter, Brian and I, as Olivia took pictures with the other band members, a playful exchange that quickly turned into heated glances and lingering hugs and small touches. As the night stretched on, this guitarist, Brian, suggested us to linger longer, I couldn't refuse. Olivia was cautious, but she stayed as well, mingling with the other band members and their associates, while I stayed close to Brian. He led me to a more secluded area of the bar as he drew me close, his faint breath, cool, against my ear. I was extremely nervous, yet calm. I had imagined this moment for several months now, yet I was still in shock that it was finally happening. He whispered with a low voice, secrets that seemed to dance in the air like fireflies. When he finally confessed the truth to me, I thought he was only teasing, he admitted to being a vampire, an immortal. The mere truth that he was more than just a man, and he was being serious, no jesting. He assured me that I was the first one he had ever confessed this to, that there was something different about me, and he hadn't stopped thinking of me since that first show last year when he first noticed me in the crowd. Honesty or not, my heart soared and somewhat plummeted all with the same breath. The mere notion of him being an actual vampire was overwhelming.

Brian began kissing my neck slowly as he mumbled, "I can make you what I am, if you want it bad enough."

The mere notion of becoming a vampire swirled in my thoughts, it was exhilarating during this heated moment of passion that I was feeling. To be like him, to share his world, whatever it may be, meant becoming one with him. It meant becoming an actual vampire, and I believe, this guy was serious. As he kissed my lips hard, the mere thrill surging throughout my body found it too powerful to resist, the allure of passion and immortality was intoxicating. So, I completely surrendered my mere being, my heart, my life, to the promise of forever.

Over the next several nights, Brian stayed in the French Quarter somewhere, and we met each night as he showed me how to feed and be a proper vampire. Of course, I tried to confess all this to Olivia, but she thought I was living in a fantasy, obsessed world. As quickly as the romance with Brian had started, it quickly turned into a nightmare. The passion that had sparked between us ignited into utter chaos. Brian's selfish darkness seemed to consume him, revealing a side that was both beautiful and very terrifying...

But, before I talk about that... the night he had actually changed me to immortality, I felt a bold hunger for blood as my mere humanity slipped away like sand through my fingers. The rush of his blood and eternity surged through my veins, yet it was not the sweet release I had hoped it to be. It was more like a curse wrapped in such seduction. My days turned only into nights, filled with bloodlust and confusion. Olivia, always by my side during the day as I slept behind closed, thick curtains that shielded me from the sun, was just as confused. She tried to anchor me, helping me, yet she believed me to be sick with some type of illness. After the first few nights of struggling with my fading humanity, I finally embraced my immortality that Brian had given me, my new existence, it was real. I was now an immortal.

As I said, our relationship became a nightmare... The thrill of immortality fading, overshadowed by the weight of my immature choices. The intoxicating, few nights with Brian were amazing, as he showed me ways to feed on a human being and only take enough blood to survive and satisfy me. Then it all turned into a blurred haze of mere desire and some regret. In a moment of desperation and slight confusion, driven by the very darkness that ensnared me, I witnessed Brian as he took a person's life. It threw me into a major whirlwind, as I still clung to my humanity, or what was left of it. After I saw him drop this being to the cold, cobblestone street, I confronted him, angered and frightful at what I just saw him do. Our relationship, once seemingly like a beacon of some kind of hope, or love, became a transformation of hate, a violent storm. We argued fiercely as he tried to assure me that we were mere killers by nature, that all this was normal for our kind as vampires. I disagreed.

In the mere chaos of our argument, I did not realize my own immortal strength and what a vampire fully consisted of, I killed Brian. After becoming so enraged, I swiftly sank my new fangs into his neck draining him dry, and snapping his undead neck afterwards, leaving him alone to burn in the rising sun that was peaking in the sky above. As I watched from the secluded, dark alleyway, I saw his ashes fly into the brightly lit sky. I remained hidden in this alley until nightfall. The actual act of taking Brian's undead life was liberating to me, yet devastating, as I still picture his immortal body crumpled on the street. I realize now the depth of my loss, I could've learned so much from him, but now it was too late. The once intoxicating vampire, the lead guitarist, I had fallen for was gone, leaving behind a small ray of guilt, a hollow ache in my undead chest, an emptiness that would echo through my endless existence.

I dwelled in my own eternal sorrow now, as I stood in the memory of something that had once been so beautiful, feeling the weight of my cruel actions, the mere evilness of what I had become, of what I had hated Brian for being. Olivia, still fully human and filled with much concern, rushed to my side, as I entered our apartment. She seen the blood that was still stained across my lips, Brian's immortal blood, "What have you done, Scarlett Anne?" she cried, much fear flashing across her face, never mind, I don't want to know."

I was too lost in my own selfish sorrow to even answer her, my heart broken, heavy with the knowledge that I had become both a predator and the prey in this estranged eternal game. Finally, I answered her and confessed the entire situation to her, even though, she said she did not want to know about it. At first, Olivia thought I was boasting, but she finally accepted the truth, when she saw the seriousness in my eyes. In shock, she almost cried, but it was her that snapped me back to my reality, my composure, "Scarlett Anne, quit feeling sorry for yourself, what is done, is done. We will move pass this and start fresh, new. Now, be the immortal you are meant to be and let's get on with our lives. At least, there is no body left behind for the authorities to find."

As the months flew by, reports of the lead guitarist that went missing was floating all across the social waves. No one knew exactly why he had disappeared, and the rumors of his immortality resurfaced into a mysterious disappearance. The band Bloody Stains continued to play and tour in his honor as they replaced his role with a new guitarist. Olivia and I never again went to their shows. We only ventured to local shows with bands that were not so famous. Now, as the moon hung high in the velvet sky over the French Quarter, I faced an uncertain future, together with Olivia, I wandered through these streets of New Orleans, just a specter of the life I once knew. Bound by a shared past, Olivia and I were just two souls, although one of us was immortal, adrift in a world where time had no meaning anymore. With every undead heartbeat, I felt the weight of my eternity continuously pressing down on me, the mere loss of Brian forever haunting my thoughts, etched into my mere being.

As we roamed nightly through the city, I found much solace in Olivia's unwavering friendship. Despite my immortal, tragic fate, I discovered that the bond that Olivia and I shared transcended the darkness surrounding me. We would navigate the shadows together, seeking purpose in our endless nights, and though forever seemed too long, we would face it side by side, two kindred spirits lost in the labyrinth of an immortal life. I shall one day, change Olivia into what I am, when she finally accepts, and is ready, until then, I will always be by her side. This small conversation still lingers in my mind, even now, as I think back at the words Olivia had said, as we were returning one late night just before sunrise from an amateur rock show...

It was a seemingly peaceful night, beneath the full moon, the city's dimly lit streets unfolded before us, the only sounds were the whispers of the howling wind and the echo of our footsteps as we walked side by side... "You know, these nights never feel quite so endless when I am with you, Scarlett Anne," Olivia stated, as she glanced up at the moonlight illuminating the cobblestone path. "It's as if time slows way down, but in a good way... like we are in a world all our own."

Smiling softly, my eyes hollow, yet glowing in the moonlight, I responded, "If there's one thing that this immortality has taught me, it's that time is only an illusion, but yes... with you, it somehow feels different now. More bearable, it seems, perhaps... You bring light to my eternal darkness, Olivia."

With a short pause of silence, as my gaze drifts toward her, Olivia, though blushing slightly, with a rare warmth in her fragile eyes, said, "I'm not sure that I bring light, but I think... I think I do help you remember what it's like to be human, feel alive, don't I?"

Nodding slowly, as I smiled, "Yes... far more than you know, Olivia. Even in the midst of my cursed fate, your very presence brings a sense of solace that I never thought I'd find again. You are... the only thing tethering me to a semblance of humanity."

With a playful, shy grin, Olivia said in response, "Tethering, huh? I will take that as a nice compliment, but you know, I do worry sometimes. You talk about your immortal curse, your mere immortality... it seems so heavy, and I just wish I could take some of that burden from you."

I paused, turning to face her, shadows playing across my pale features, "Perhaps one day, you might, Olivia. There is a way... a way for us to truly share everything, to always be together. You just have to become like me, a vampire, immortal, but that's a choice only you can decide when the time comes. Until then..." I reached out, brushing a strand of her long, blonde hair from her face, "I will continue to walk by your side, for as long as you will have me."

Olivia's emerald eyes widened, a mixture of much curiosity and hesitation, "You mean... you'd actually turn me, if I asked you to? But what if I never ask? What if I'm not ready? Will you... grow tired of waiting?"

Shaking my head, my voice soft and resolute, "Never, Olivia. Immortality may be a curse, but it does have its qualities. It has taught me a lot about patience. If forever is the time it takes for you to decide, then forever I shall wait. I would rather wander the dark with you as you are now, than face an eternity without you."

Looking down, a small hunt of sadness in her voice, Olivia said, "I'm afraid, you know. Afraid of losing who I truly am, what little life I have, what little faith I have, but at the same time... the mere thought of watching you drift away from my life, leaving me behind as I grow into an old woman... that is what terrifies me the most."

Stepping closer to her, taking her hands in mine, her touch warm yet comforting against my cold fingers, "The decision is yours, Olivia, it always will be. Immortality does change everything, especially how you believe, but some things, some bonds, they remain. What we have... our friendship... it's one of those rare things that can truly endure even in the shadows of eternity. Until then, we will keep searching, living life together, finding purpose in these seemingly endless nights."

Smiling through the mist of unshed tears, she said, "I'm not sure what the future may hold for us, but I do know one thing... I am not ready to let you go, so, let's keep wandering, my friend, my immortal guide, my sister in this vast world, this unknown darkness."

Smiling, my voice as soft as a whisper, "Always, Olivia. Until the stars fall from the sky and the darkness swallows the sun... I will be right here, right by your side. Now, enough emotional talk... let's discuss how cute that bass player looked in his tight jeans tonight."

Arm and arm, we made our way to our small apartment before the sun began to show in the night's sky. My thoughts were swirling with the mere reality that Olivia and I would always continue to proceed on our journey through this city, night after night, just two souls bound by cruel fate, enduring the shadows of darkness together, knowing that no matter what our future throws at us now, we would face it together, side by side. Just a mere party that would last forever between us.

Many years passed since that fateful night that I took Brian's undead life. I can still hear the echoes of his guitar lingering in the night air, a bittersweet reminder of a romance that once burned with passion. I learned to embrace the depths of my mere existence while still dwelling here in the French Quarter. I learned to transform the pain of loss and regret, the guilt, into a fierce determination to protect those I loved, which was Olivia. As New Orleans remained our playground, a city where every street corner held many memories of laughter and music, I avoided that one particular street where Brian's ashes had faded away.

In the end Olivia and I carved our own path, celebrating our friendship, our deep bond, amidst the darkness that I always seemed to carry. We would dance under the moonlight within the French Quarter, as we would always sing along to our favorite rock songs, and carry the legacy of my tragic love story, though brief, within our hearts forever. I eventually transformed Olivia into this immortality. We remain together, inseparable, as we continue our journey, our legacy, within the French Quarter.

In the vast eternity of my undead life, I found that sorrow, the mere threads of such a connection, could weave a tapestry of slight hope, a small reminder that love, passion, though fleeting, could echo through time, through the ages. The mere thought crosses my mind, 'So, it was true, Brian was a vampire...'

Forever Seems Too Long

The End.

Forever Seems Too Long

By Jo Ann Atcheson Gray

Life can be fun and interesting!
I'm Scarlett Anne. I am now immortal.
This is my tragic Love story of how I found love and how it was destroyed.
Sometimes the 'Party' isn't as much fun as it would seem when Forever seems too long!